Assessment Papers

First papers in English

J M Bond

and Sarah Lindsay

Nelson Thornes
a Wolters Kluwer business

First published in 1973 by:
Thomas Nelson and Sons Ltd

This edition published in 2007 by:
Nelson Thornes Ltd
Delta Place
27 Bath Road
CHELTENHAM
GL53 7TH
United Kingdom

07 08 09 10 11 / 10 9 8 7 6 5 4 3 2 1

A catalogue record for this book is available from the British Library

ISBN 978 0 7487 8105 8

Illustrations by Nigel Kitching and R. Barton and K. Kett
Page make-up by GreenGate Publishing Services, Tonbridge, Kent

Printed and bound in Croatia by Zrinski

Acknowledgements

The authors and publishers wish to thank the following for permission to use
copyright material:

Extract from *Bill's New Frock* by Anne Fine, copyright © Anne Fine 2002,
reproduced by permission of Egmont Books Ltd; extract from 'The Unknown
Planet' by Jean Ure, copyright © Jean Ure 1992, first published by Walker
Books in 1992, and reproduced by permission of the author c/o The Maggie
Noach Literary Agency; 'Daddy fell into the Pond' by Alfred Noyes, reproduced
by permission of the Society of Authors as the literary representative of the
Estate of Alfred Noyes; extract from *Farm Boy* by Michael Morpurgo, Collins
1997, reproduced by permission of Pavilion Books; extract from *BBC Fact
finders: The Vikings* by Peter Chrisp © 1993, reproduced by permission of
Pearson Education; 'Dinosaur Stomp' by David Harmer; extract from *Chicken
Mission* by Sue Limb copyright © 1988, reproduced by permission of Hachette
Children's Books; extract from *The Shining Princess* by Eric Quayle and Michael
Foreman, copyright © 1989, reproduced by permission of Anderson Press Ltd;
extract from 'The Spider and the Lion' in *Tales from Africa* retold by Kathleen
Arnott (OUP, 2000), copyright © Kathleen Arnott 1962, reprinted by permission
of Oxford University Press; extract from *A sudden Swirl of Icy Wind* by Anne
Fine, copyright © 1990, Piccadilly Press.

Every effort has been made to trace the copyright holders, but if any have been
inadvertently overlooked the publishers will be pleased to make the necessary
arrangement at the first opportunity.

Before you get started

What is Bond?

This book is part of the Bond Assessment Papers series for English, which provides **thorough and continuous practice of key English skills** from ages five to thirteen. Bond's English resources are ideal preparation for many different kinds of tests and exams – from SATs to 11+ and other secondary school selection exams.

What does this book cover?

It practises comprehension, spelling, grammar, punctuation and vocabulary work appropriate for children of this age. It is fully in line with the National Curriculum for English and the National Literacy Strategy. One of the key features of Bond Assessment Papers is that each one practises **a wide variety of skills and question types** so that children are always challenged to think – and don't get bored repeating the same question type again and again. We think that variety is the key to effective learning. It helps children 'think on their feet' and cope with the unexpected.

The age given on the cover is for guidance only. As the papers are designed to be reasonably challenging for the age group, any one child may naturally find him or herself working above or below the stated age. The important thing is that children are always encouraged by their performance. Working at the right level is the key to this.

What does the book contain?

- **20 papers** – each one contains 30 questions.

- **Scoring devices** – there are score boxes in the margins and a Progress Chart on page 60. The chart is a visual and motivating way for children to see how they are doing. Encouraging them to colour in the chart as they go along and to try to beat their last score can be highly effective!

- **Next Steps** – advice on what to do after finishing the papers can be found on the inside back cover.

- **Answers** – located in an easily-removed central pull-out section. If you lose your answers, please email cservices@ nelsonthornes.com for another copy.

- **Key English words** – on page 1 you will find a glossary of special key words that are used in the papers. These are highlighted in bold each time that they appear. These words are now used in the English curriculum and children are expected to know them at this age.

How can you use this book?

One of the great strengths of Bond Assessment Papers is their flexibility. They can be used at home, school and by tutors to:

- provide regular English practice in **bite-sized chunks**

- **highlight strengths and weaknesses** in the core skills

- identify **individual needs**

- set **homework**

- set **timed formal practice** tests – allow about 30 minutes.

It is best to start at the beginning and work through the papers in order.

What does a score mean and how can it be improved?

If children colour in the Progress Chart at the back, this will give an idea of how they are doing. The Next Steps inside the back cover will help you to decide what to do next to help a child progress. We suggest that it is always valuable to go over any wrong answers with children.

Don't forget the website…!

Visit www.assessmentpapers.co.uk for lots of advice, information and suggestions on everything to do with Bond and helping children to do their best.

Key words

Some special words are used in this book. You will find them in **bold** each time they appear in the Papers. These words are explained here.

adjective   a word that describes somebody or something

alphabetical order   words arranged in the order found in the alphabet

antonym   a word with a meaning opposite to another word *hot – cold*

collective noun   a word referring to a group   *swarm*

compound word   a word made up of two other words   *football*

conjunction   a word used to link sentences, phrases and words *and*, *but*

consonant letters   all letters of the alphabet apart from a, e, i, o, u (vowel letters)

definition   a meaning of a word

dialogue word   a word used for the way people say things   *shouted*

diminutive   a word implying smallness   *booklet*

homonym   a word that has the same spelling as another word, but a different meaning

noun   a word for somebody or something

past tense   form of a verb showing something that has already happened

personal pronoun   a pronoun used when writing about ourselves or others   *I*, *you*, *he*

plural   more than one   *cats*

possessive pronoun   a pronoun used to tell us who owns something   *his*, *mine*

prefix   a group of letters added to the beginning of a word *un*, *dis*

present tense   form of a verb showing something happening now

pronoun   a word often replacing a noun

root word   a word to which prefixes or suffixes can be added to make other words   *quickly*

singular   one   *cat*

suffix   a group of letters added to the end of a word   *ly*, *ful*

synonym   a word with the same or very similar meaning to another word   *quick – fast*

verb   a 'doing' or 'being' word

vowel letters   the letters a, e, i, o, u

One day a farmer was out in the fields when he heard a rumble of thunder.

'I've just about had enough of you, Thunder God!' he shouted. 'I know you send down thunder and rain just to upset me.' He cursed the god. 'Come and get me!' he yelled. 'I'm ready for you!'

The farmer hung a great big iron cage outside his house. 5

'Stay inside the house until I tell you to come out,' he ordered his son and daughter. 'There's some serious fighting to be done.'

The Thunder God had heard the farmer's cursing and was angry with him, so – with a mighty crash of thunder and a brilliant flash of lightning – he appeared above the farm house. 10

'Come down here and face me, you coward!' yelled the angry farmer. 'Don't stay up there in the clouds.'

So the Thunder God came crashing down to Earth, clutching an enormous battle axe. The farmer only had an iron fork he used in the field, but he also had the advantage. He was used to standing on the 15 ground and on his own two feet, and was ready and waiting for this god who was shaking with rage.

With one swift movement the farmer caught him on the prongs of the fork. Before the god knew what was happening, he was flipped into the cage and the door slammed shut. 20

'There!' said the farmer triumphantly. 'You can rumble and rage as much as you like now, but you can't bother me.' Soon the rain stopped and the clouds cleared. The god had been defeated.

Next morning, the farmer decided to go to market to buy some herbs.

'I think I'm going to pickle the Thunder God for all to see,' he told 25 his daughter. 'You must stay well clear of the cage and don't talk to the Thunder God, whatever he might say to frighten you,' he insisted. 'And most importantly of all,' he added, with a stern face, 'you must not give him a drink.'

From *Chinese Myths and Legends* by Philip Ardagh

Underline the right answers.

1 Why was the farmer angry with the Thunder God?
(he was too big, he sent down thunder and rain, he was too noisy)

2 What weapon did the farmer have?
(a sword, a battle axe, an iron fork)

3 Where did the farmer go the next morning?
(to market, to his fields, to the river)

4 Which was the most important order the farmer gave to his children?
(not to go near the cage, not to give the Thunder God a drink, not to talk to him)

4

Answer these questions.

5 What advantage did the farmer have over the Thunder God?

_____

_____

6 How did the farmer feel after capturing the Thunder God?

_____

_____

7 What happened to the weather after the Thunder God was trapped?

_____

_____

8 Why did the farmer go to market?

_____

_____

9 What do you think might happen if the Thunder God were given a drink?

_____

_____

5

Add *ing* to the word at the beginning of each line and use it to finish the sentence.

10 **help**   I am _____ to wash up.

11 **play**   She was _____ with her toys.

12 **fly**   The plane was _____ overhead.

13 **wear**   Tara was _____ her best dress.

14 **kick**   Tom was _____ the ball.

15 **read**   The children were _____ their books.   **6**

Circle the **vowel letters** in these words.

16 tennis   17 football   18 rowing   **3**

Write out these sentences putting in the capital letters and full stops.

19–20 the holiday was great

_____

21–22 the dog swam across the river

_____   **4**

Put these words in the order you would find them in a dictionary.

cat   horse   pig   rat   dog

23 (1) _____   24 (2) _____   25 (3) _____

26 (4) _____   27 (5) _____   **5**

Circle the **consonant letters** in these words.

28 pencil   29 ruler   30 rubber   **3**

When Bill Simpson woke up on Monday morning, he found he was a girl.

He was still standing staring at himself in the mirror, quite baffled, when his mother swept in.

'Why don't you wear this pretty pink dress?' she said.

'I *never* wear dresses,' Bill burst out. 5

'I know,' his mother said. 'It's such a pity.'

And, to his astonishment, before he could even begin to argue, she had dropped the dress over his head and zipped up the back.

'I'll leave you to do up the shell buttons,' she said. 'They're a bit fiddly and I'm late for work.' 10

And she swept out leaving him staring in dismay at the mirror. In it, a girl with his curly red hair and wearing a pretty pink frock with fiddly shell buttons was staring back at him in equal dismay.

'This can't be true,' Bill Simpson said to himself. 'This cannot be true!'

He stepped out of his bedroom just as his father was rushing past. He, 15
too, was late in getting off to work.

Mr Simpson leaned over and planted a kiss on Bill's cheek.

'Bye, Poppet,' he said, ruffling Bill's curls. 'You look very sweet today. It's not often we see you in a frock, is it?'

He ran down the stairs and out of the house so quickly he didn't see 20
Bill's scowl, or hear what he muttered savagely under his breath.

Bella the cat didn't seem to notice any difference. She purred and rubbed her soft, furry body around his ankles in exactly the same way she always did.

From *Bill's New Frock* by Anne Fine

Underline the right answers.

1 How was the dress fastened?
(by buttons, by a zip, by a zip and buttons)

2 Bill's dad was late for (the train, work, the bus).

3 Why did Bill's mum not do the buttons up?
(so Bill could practise doing up buttons, because she was late for work, because there was a zip)

4 The cat was called (Poppet, Bella, Felix).

4

Answer these questions.

5 What does 'baffled' mean in line 2?

_____

6 What was Bill's hair like?

_____

7 How did Bill react to being kissed by his dad?

_____

8–9 What two things did the cat usually do when she saw Bill?

(1) _____

(2) _____

10 Say in your own words what was odd about the behaviour of Bill's mum and dad.

_____

_____

_____

6

Read the clues to help find the words ending in *le*.

11 You can blow it out. ca_____

12 Do this to eggs and put it on toast. scr_____

13 It is just above your foot. a_____

14 Nearly a fall. stu_____

4

Some of the words below should begin with a capital letter. Rewrite them correctly.

15–20 john and his dog smudge went to brighton for the day last sunday. the weather was warm although it was march.

_____   _____   _____

_____   _____   _____   ⟩ 6

Add a question mark (?) or full stop to each of these sentences.

21 I like beefburgers

22 Where is it

23 Open the door

24 May I have some

25 Is it raining   ⟩ 5

Write a word which means the opposite of each word.

26 big   _____   **27** old   _____

28 early   _____   **29** quick   _____

30 wet   _____   ⟩ 5

51 Low Road
Tavistock
Devon
DX1 6AH

2 April   5

Dear Mrs Crebbins

I'm so sorry about what happened to the garden yesterday. We really didn't mean to cause all that damage.

What happened was, I was leading 9–2 when Simon tried a long range shot. It did miss, by quite a lot, and went flying over the fence towards your conservatory. There was a bit of a crash.   10

I know you did tell us not to come round for our ball after last week. My dad will be fixing the greenhouse soon. Anyway I was Brazil and Simon was England and it was only half-time so it seemed a shame not to finish the game. There was a hole   15
in your hedge to get through but Simon is quite big for his age. He does like chips rather a lot. Anyway he got stuck. I got Mum's clippers to make the hole just a bit bigger (though I might have overdone it). Simon got through and grabbed the ball when Snooker came running down your garden. He was   20
barking like a werewolf. Simon tried to hurl the ball back over but it hit the greenhouse again. Then he climbed up your new small tree. When they both crashed to the ground Snooker grabbed Simon by the leg.

I threw a stone at Snooker and he ran away. Simon couldn't   25
walk so he had to crawl through your flowerbed back to the hedge. I think some of the flowers survived. I then had to make another hole in the hedge to get Simon back.

I am very sorry about all this. My dad says we can't play football any more. Anyway it's nearly the cricket season. I'm   30
going to be India.

Best wishes

Sanjay
P.S. I think Simon's dad is going to the police about the bites.

Underline the right answers.

1 Sanjay was pretending to be (India, Brazil, England).

2 Last week the boys damaged (the greenhouse, the lawn, the conservatory).

3 Why did Simon crawl back to the hedge?
(to avoid Mrs Crebbins, to avoid Snooker, because his leg had been bitten)

3

Answer these questions.

4 How do you know that Simon is not very good at football?

_____

_____

5 Write down four things that were damaged in the game.

(1) _____   (2) _____

(3) _____   (4) _____

6 Why was Simon too big to get through the hole in the hedge?

_____

7 Why will Mrs Crebbins' garden continue to be in danger after the football game?

_____

8 How did Simon's dad feel about the situation?

_____

_____

5

Put commas in the right places.

9–11 I like apples grapes plums peaches and pears.

12–13 Shall we play on the swing slide climbing frame and roundabout?

14–15 Jason collects ladybirds ants spiders and centipedes.

7

Underline the two words in each line which have similar meanings.

16–17 large   small   big

18–19 hard   easy   simple

20–21 weep   shout   sob

6

Write the **singular** of each of these words.

22 cows   _____   23 roads   _____

24 shoes   _____   25 bananas   _____

26 footballs   _____

5

Circle the **verb** in each sentence.

27 James plunged into the water.

28 Clare crept past the door.

29 Dan sprinted to the finish line.

30 Alice crawled into the kitchen.

4

Now go to the Progress Chart to record your score!   Total   **30**

Our activity trip

Last weekend we went for an activity weekend at the Wyefield Activity Centre. There were two classes from our school, and two from Highpark Junior. I shared a room with Sharon and Jane and two girls from Highpark, Susie and Beth. I was a bit worried about sharing with girls I didn't know but we soon got on fine.

5

On Friday we went to the mining museum and saw how they used to mine coal there. It was so dark and spooky in the mine. After a picnic lunch we went canoeing on the Wye. We were shown how to paddle and given lifejackets, then we set off in the rain! It was good fun, but hard work. At first we just went round in circles, then we got the hang of it, but I was glad to see the minibus. Mike and Imran were best at canoeing. Susie and Beth had to be towed by Mr Thompson.

10

15

Supper was pretty good then we watched a DVD. We stayed up talking in bed really late, until Mrs Wiggins came round and told us off! I was pretty tired the next morning. Still the morning trip to the leisure centre was amazing. The water slides were the best ever. The double flume was amazing, like shooting the rapids in a real river. You swooshed down incredibly fast. I must have gone down a dozen times.

20

I must admit I was a bit tired out for the last part of the trip, the survey of Wentbury Castle. The castle was right on the top of the hill, surrounded by a deep ditch. Some of the walls were a bit bashed down but most of it was still there. Not bad, as it was built in the Middle Ages! You could imagine knights clanking over the drawbridge in their armour. I hope they had good fires. It was cold and windy and the rain pelted down just before we got onto the bus again. It was a great two days but I was really glad to be home again. The best bit was the leisure centre. The worst was the rain. Thank goodness we had our wellies and macs!

25

30

Bryony Phillips, Lowbury Junior School

35

Underline the right answers.

1 Which of these girls went to Lowbury School?
(Susie, Beth, Bryony, Jane)

2 Why did Mrs Wiggins tell the girls off?
(for talking late, for running about, for eating in bed)

3 Wentbury Castle was built in which period?
(Victorian times, Tudor times, the Middle Ages)

Answer these questions.

4 What was Bryony worried about before going?

_____

5 List in order the four places that the schools went to on their trip.

(1) _____   (2) _____

(3) _____   (4) _____

6 Which place did Bryony enjoy most and why?

_____

_____

7 Say in your own words why you think Bryony would not have enjoyed living in the Middle Ages.

_____

_____

Add the **prefix** *un* to the words in bold to make their **antonyms** (a word with an opposite meaning).

8 Shaun is not **happy**. He is _____.

9 The wicked witch was not **kind**. She was _____.

10 The spaceman was not **afraid**. He was _____.

11 The teacher is not **fair**. She is _____.

12 Those shelves are not **tidy**. They are _____.

13 The fish have not been **cooked**. They are _____.

3

4

6

Finish these sentences in your own words.

14 It was dark when _____

15 I wish I was still in bed but _____

16 I'm early because _____

17 Shout loudly and _____   4

With a line match each word with its **definition**.

18 midnight   a feeling of fondness

19 diamond   middle of the night

20 starling   a common European bird

21 affection   a line of people

22 umbrella   a shelter from the rain

23 queue   a hard precious stone   6

Underline the **singular nouns** and circle the **plural nouns**.

24 bushes   25 monster   26 bus

27 churches   28 knives   29–30 fish   7

Now go to the Progress Chart to record your score!   Total   30

Shimma's head felt as though it were bursting. Through the porthole she could see stars whizzing and whirling, making dizzying patterns in the sky.

The ship was spinning, out of control. Over and over, it tumbled through space. The next minute and – CRASH! The whole ship juddered as it hit something hard. At the same time came the shrill screaming of the hooter – *aahwaa*, *aahwaa*, *aahwaa*! Everyone knew what that meant: Danger! Abandon ship!

With shaking hands, Shimma fumbled for the clasp which would release her. She felt herself jerked upright by Finn and bundled towards the exit. Already the emergency hatches were sliding open ...

The passengers and crew of the stricken *Sea Queen* stood huddled together for comfort. The lights from their helmets showed that the ship had landed on a vast expanse of rock, flat and bare as far as the eye could see. Shimma reached out for Finn's hand. 'Don't worry,' he said. 'They'll soon have her working again. We shan't be here long.'

The Captain was just giving his orders – 'Unload the space-hoppers! Get them clear of the ship!' – when out of the blackness came a loud and hideous roaring and the ground began to tremble at their feet.

Even as they stood there, not knowing which way to run for safety, the thing leapt at them. Over the rim of the rocky plateau it came, snorting and bellowing, jaws gaping wide, yellow eyes glowing like twin suns in the darkness.

From *The Unknown Planet* by Jean Ure

Underline the right answers.

1 What clue did Shimma have that the ship was out of control?
(the captain said so, the stars were making unusual patterns, the engine had stopped)

2 Who helped Shimma out of the space ship?
(Finn, no one, the Captain)

3 The ship crashed on (a muddy place, a cold place, a rocky place).

◯ 3

Answer these questions.

4 How can you tell Shimma is frightened after the hooter goes?

_____

5 The writer says the ship is 'stricken' in line 11. What does 'stricken' mean?

_____

6 How do the passengers see in the dark?

_____

7 What did Finn think would happen after they landed?

_____

8 What were the eyes of 'the thing' like?

_____

9–10 Give two reasons for thinking that 'the thing' was dangerous.

(1) _____

(2) _____

◯ 7

Write out these sentences, putting capital letters in the right places.

11–13 ben and his friend went to london last thursday.

_____

14–18 they went to london zoo and oxford street.

_____

◯ 8

15

Complete the table.

19–23

	+er	+est
cold	colder	
tall		
fast		

5

Underline the **dialogue words** (the words used for the way people say things) in these sentences.

24 "Help, I'm stuck in the mud!" screamed Nasar.

25 "Where are you going?" Miss Thornton asked.

26 "Look at the clown!" giggled Caroline.

27 "I can't find my swimming costume," Joe complained.

4

Add another **verb** with a similar meaning to each group.

28 run, chase, _____

29 eat, gobble, _____

30 shout, scream, _____

3

Now go to the Progress Chart to record your score!   Total 30

16

Paper 6

Daddy fell into the Pond

Everyone grumbled. The sky was grey.
We had nothing to do and nothing to say.
We were nearing the end of a dismal day.
And there seemed to be nothing beyond,
THEN DADDY FELL INTO THE POND!   5
And everyone's face grew merry and bright,
And Timothy danced for sheer delight.
"Give me the camera, quick, oh quick!
He's crawling out of the duckweed!" Click!
Then the gardener suddenly slapped his knee, 10
And doubled up, shaking silently,
The ducks all quacked as if they were daft,
And it sounded as if the old drake laughed.
Oh, there wasn't a thing that didn't respond
WHEN DADDY FELL INTO THE POND!   15

by Alfred Noyes

Underline the right answers.

1 At first they were all (happy, busy, moaning).

2 They had nothing to do and nothing to (play, say, watch).

3 The weather was (wet, sunny, cloudy).

4 What did Timothy do when Daddy fell into the pond?
(laughed, danced, grumbled)

4

Answer these questions.

5 Who do you think took the picture of Daddy in the pond?

_____

6 Why do you think the gardener was shaking?

_____

7 Why do you think 'it sounded as if the old drake [male duck] laughed'?

_____

8 How do you think Daddy felt?

_____

4

Two words on each line are **synonyms** (they are words with similar meanings). Underline them.

9–10 large   small   little

11–12 quick   slow   fast

13–14 sea   ocean   beach

6

Choose one of the **adjectives** to fill each space.

bright   sharp   scary   rough   rainy

15 _____ light   16 _____ pencil

17 _____ day   18 _____ film

19 _____ sea

5

Rewrite the passage, putting in the missing punctuation and capital letters.

20–26 mum said that she would take paul to london to buy some roller skates they set off from walton at nine o'clock

_____

_____

_____

7

Use the pictures to help finish the **compound words**.

27 snow + = _____

28 sea + = _____

29 pine + = _____

30 foot + = _____

4

A recipe for sticky toffee banana pudding

Serves 4 people

You need
¼ cup butter
1 cup brown sugar
1 tablespoon lemon juice
4 thick slices of brown bread
4 bananas, cut into chunks

How to make it
Melt the butter in a large frying pan. Don't make the pan too hot.
Add sugar and lemon juice. Stir until the sugar melts. Turn the heat down low. You now have the toffee mixture.
Remove the crusts from the bread and cut into chunks. Stir the bread into the mixture until it is evenly covered all over.
Add the bananas. Stir gently. Cover the pan. Let it cook for 4 minutes. The bananas should be soft but don't let them get too mushy.
You can serve it hot or cold. If you serve it cold put it in the fridge for a short while before serving.

Underline the right answers.

1 What ingredients make the toffee mixture?
   (lemon juice and sugar, butter and lemon juice, sugar and butter and lemon juice)

Answer these questions.

2–3 What two things does the recipe tell you not to do?

_____

_____

4 What must you do to the bread at the start?

_____

5 Why do you think it is important to cover the bread evenly all over?

_____

6 How many bananas would you need if you were making this recipe for six people?

_____

7 What should you do if you want to eat the pudding cold?

_____

⎯ 6

Write four more words ending in the _ly_ **suffix**.

8–11 quickly _____ _____ _____

_____

⎯ 4

Add the missing speech marks (" ") to these sentences.

12 Where are you going? called Mum.

13 Here we are, Tom shouted.

14 It is over there! yelled Sarah.

15 Shh, Tuhil is asleep, Dad whispered.

16 Quick, it is catching us! Gemma screamed.

⎯ 5

Write the **plural** of each of these **nouns**.

17 gate _____ **18** track _____

19 bridge _____ **20** rabbit _____

21 tractor _____ **22** farm _____

⎯ 6

Each of these words has two meanings. Write the numbers of the two meanings that match each word.

23–24 wave ____ ____ **25–26** duck ____ ____

27–28 tank ____ ____ **29–30** stick ____ ____

(1) a bird which swims (2) a twig

(3) an arm movement (4) to glue

(5) machinery used by the army (6) to dip your head quickly

(7) movement of water (8) a home for fish in the house

⎯ 8

Paper 8

'Tell us a story!' said the March Hare.

'Yes, please do!' pleaded Alice.

'And be quick about it,' added the Hatter, 'or you'll be asleep again before it's done.'

'Once upon a time there were three little sisters,' the Dormouse began   *5*
in a great hurry; 'and their names were Elsie, Lacie, and Tillie; and they lived at the bottom of a well –'

'What did they live on?' said Alice, who always took a great interest in questions of eating and drinking.

'They lived on treacle,' said the Dormouse, after thinking a minute or   *10*
two.

'They couldn't have done that, you know,' Alice gently remarked. 'They'd have been ill.'

'So they were,' said the Dormouse; '*very* ill.'

Alice tried to fancy to herself what such an extraordinary way of living   *15*
would be like, but it puzzled her too much, so she went on, 'but why did they live at the bottom of a well?'

The Dormouse again took a minute or two to think about it, and then it said, 'It was a treacle-well.'

'There's no such thing!' Alice was beginning very angrily, but the Hatter   *20*
and the March Hare went 'Sh! Sh!' and the Dormouse sulkily remarked, 'If you can't be civil, you'd better finish the story yourself.'

'No please go on!', Alice said very humbly. 'I won't interrupt again. I dare say there may be one.'

From *Alice's Adventures in Wonderland* by Lewis Carroll

Underline the right answers.

1 Who was telling the story?
(Alice, the Hatter, the Dormouse)

2 Who was the story about?
(three sisters, three brothers, three friends)

3 Who told Alice to be quiet?
(the Dormouse and the Hatter, the March Hare and the Dormouse, the March Hare and the Hatter)

3

Answer these questions.

4–5 Write down two things in the Dormouse's story that seemed like nonsense to Alice.

_____

_____

6 The Dormouse told Alice to be 'civil' in line 22. What does civil mean?

_____

7 Why was the Dormouse getting sulky with Alice?

_____

8 Do you think Alice was enjoying the story? Why?

_____

5

Fill each gap with a **verb**.

9 Matthew _____ to the football match.

10 Mum and Dad _____ the children on holiday.

11 Jess _____ some herbs in a pot.

12 _____ behind your ears, Tim!

13 We _____ the kittens at six o'clock.

14 The cat _____ the milk.

6

Match the beginning of each sentence with its ending. Write the number.

15 A book _____   (1) can fly.

16 A fish _____   (2) boils water.

17 A plane _____   (3) can swim.

18 A wardrobe _____   (4) has branches.

19 A kettle _____   (5) can be read.

20 A tree _____   (6) holds clothes.

6

Write these words in **alphabetical order**.

helicopter   ship   train   lorry

21 (1) _____   **22** (2) _____

23 (3) _____   **24** (4) _____   4

Circle the silent letter in each word.

25 knot   **26** wrap   **27** climb

28 wriggly   **29** comb   **30** knee   6

Now go to the Progress Chart to record your score!   Total   30

23

Paper 9

Chips

Out of the paper bag
Comes the hot breath of the chips
And I shall blow on them
To stop them burning my lips.

Before I leave the counter   5
The woman shakes
Raindrops of vinegar on them
And salty snowflakes.

Outside the frosty pavements
Are slippery as a slide   10
But the chips and I
Are warm inside.

by Stanley Cook

Underline the right answers.

  1 There were (sweets, flakes, chips) in the bag.

  2 The weather was (hot, wet, frosty, snowy).

  3 The chips were in (newspaper, a paper bag, a carton).

3

Answer these questions.

  4 What did the woman put on the chips?

  _____

  5 Why did the person blow on the chips?

  _____

  6 How do we know there was ice on the pavements?

  _____

  7–9 Find three words in the poem that could also describe the weather.

  _____   _____   _____

6

24

Underline all the words which should start with a capital letter.

10–14

cat	france	kite	joke
monday	henry	purple	cupboard
highchair	india	julia	goat

5

Write the **antonym** (opposite) for each word in bold.

15 Mum says I must stay **in**. I want to go _____.

16 First I turned on the **hot** tap and then I turned on the _____ one.

17 Anne was **first**, but Sally was _____.

18 I found the question **hard** but Tom found it _____.

19 Goldilocks didn't sleep in the **big** bed, she slept in the _____ one.

5

Add the missing apostrophes (').

20 do not   = d o n t   **21** can not = c a n t

22 we have = w e v e   **23** we are   = w e r e

24 it is   = i t s   **25** did not = d i d n t

6

Circle the **adjective** or adjectives in these sentences.

26 The yellow butter melted.

27 Dad has smelly socks.

28–29 Natasha wore a long, pretty dress.

30 Henry ate the huge bar of chocolate.

5

Now go to the Progress Chart to record your score!   Total   30

Paper 10

There's an old green Fordson tractor in the back of Grandpa's barn, always covered in cornsacks. When I was little, I used to go in there, pull off the cornsacks, climb up and drive it all over the farm. I'd be gone all morning sometimes, but they always knew where to find me. I'd be ploughing or tilling or mowing, anything I wanted. It didn't matter to me that the engine didn't work, that one of the iron wheels was missing, that I couldn't even move the steering wheel. 5

Up there on my tractor, I was a farmer, like my Grandpa, and I could go all over the farm, wherever I wanted. When I'd finished, I always had to put the cornsacks back and cover it up. Grandpa said I had to, so that it didn't get dusty. That old tractor, he said, was very important, very special. I knew that already of course, but it wasn't until many years later that I discovered just how important, just how special it was. 10

I come from a family of farmers going back generations and generations, but I wouldn't have known much about it if Grandpa hadn't told me. My own mother and father never seemed that interested in family roots, or maybe they just preferred not to talk about them. My mother grew up on the farm. She was the youngest of four sisters, and none of them had stayed on the farm any longer than they'd had to. School took her to college. College took her off to London, to teaching first, then to meeting my father, a townie through and through, and one who made no secret of his dislike for the countryside and everything to do with it. 15

20

From *Farm Boy* by Michael Morpurgo

Underline the right answers.

1 Where was the tractor kept?
   (outside, in the barn, in the garage)

2 Why did he have to cover the tractor with cornsacks?
   (to stop it getting wet, to stop it getting dirty, to stop it getting dusty)

3 Why did the boy's mother first leave the farm?
   (to work, to get married, to go to college)

3

Answer these questions.

4–6 What three things might the boy do while sitting on the tractor?

_____

7 Say what 'a townie through and through' means, in your own words.

_____

8 Why do you think the boy's father was not interested in farming?

_____

Write the **collective noun** to match each picture.

herd   flock   bunch   choir

9 _____

10 _____

11 _____

12 _____

Write the expressions in the table.

Hello.   How are you?

Watch out!   Good to see you.

Mind your head!   Take care!

13–18

Expression of greeting	Expression of warning

Add the missing exclamation marks (!) or question marks (?) where they are needed.

19 Be quiet_____   **20** What is your name_____

21 Help_____   **22** Hurry up_____

23 Do you want to watch a video_____   **24** Is it big_____

6

Add the **prefixes** *un* or *dis* to each word.

25 _____even   **26** _____obey   **27** _____appear

28 _____tie   **29** _____happy   **30** _____agree

6

Now go to the Progress Chart to record your score!   Total   30

Some questions will be answered in the children's own words. Answers to these questions are given in *italics*. Any answers that seem to be in line with these should be marked correct.

Paper 1

1   he sent down thunder and rain
2   an iron fork
3   to market
4   not to give the Thunder God a drink
5   *He was used to standing on the ground and on his own two feet.*
6   *He felt triumphant/pleased.*
7   *The rain stopped and the clouds cleared.*
8   *He went to buy some herbs.*
9   *Any sensible answer that shows the child understands that something important will happen, e.g. the Thunder God will get away.*
10 helping
11 playing
12 flying
13 wearing
14 kicking
15 reading
16 tennis
17 football
18 rowing
19–20 The holiday was great.
21–22 The dog swam across the river.
23 cat
24 dog
25 horse
26 pig
27 rat
28 **pencil**
29 **ruler**
30 **rubber**

Paper 2

1   by a zip and buttons
2   work
3   because she was late for work
4   Bella
5   *Puzzled, confused.*
6   Curly and red.
7   *He was cross/he scowled/he muttered under his breath.*
8   *She purred.*
9   *She rubbed herself against Bill's ankles.*
10 *Any answer that suggests that they thought that wearing a dress was quite normal for Bill e.g. The behaviour of Bill's mum and dad was very strange, as they seemed to think it was perfectly normal for him to wear a dress.*
11 candle
12 scramble
13 ankle
14 stumble
15–20 John Smudge Brighton Sunday The March
21 I like beefburgers.
22 Where is it?
23 Open the door.
24 May I have some?
25 Is it raining?
26 *little/small*
27 *young/new*
28 *late*
29 *slow*
30 *dry*

Paper 3

1   Brazil
2   the greenhouse
3   because his leg had been bitten
4   *Either because he was losing 9–2 or because his shot missed by a long way.*
5   *Four of: the hedge, the conservatory, the tree, the greenhouse, the flowerbed, Simon's leg.*
6   *He liked chips rather a lot.*

7 *The boys will soon be playing cricket.*

8 *Any answer that suggests he was angry, e.g. Simon's dad was so angry he was considering going to the police about the bites.*

9–11 I like apples, grapes, plums, peaches and pears.

12–13 Shall we play on the swing, slide, climbing frame and roundabout?

14 Jason collects ladybirds, ants, spiders and centipedes.

16–17 <u>large</u>   small   <u>big</u>

18–19 hard   <u>easy</u>   <u>simple</u>

20–21 <u>weep</u>   shout   <u>sob</u>

22 cow

23 road

24 shoe

25 banana

26 football

27 plunged

28 crept

29 sprinted

30 crawled

Paper 4

1 Bryony, Jane

2 for talking late

3 the Middle Ages

4 *She was worried about sharing a room with girls she didn't know.*

5 (1) the mining museum, (2) canoeing on the Wye, (3) the leisure centre, (4) Wentbury Castle

6 *She liked the leisure centre because the water slides were very good.*

7 *It was uncomfortable and cold.*

8 unhappy

9 unkind

10 unafraid

11 unfair

12 untidy

13 uncooked

14–17 *Sentences finished in own words, e.g. It was dark when I got up for school.*

18 midnight – middle of the night

19 diamond – a hard precious stone

20 starling – a common European bird

21 affection – a feeling of fondness

22 umbrella – a shelter from the rain

23 queue – a line of people

24 **bushes**

25 <u>monster</u>

26 <u>bus</u>

27 **churches**

28 **knives**

29–30 <u>fish</u>

Paper 5

1 the stars were making unusual patterns

2 Finn

3 A rocky place

4 *Her hands were shaking.*

5 *The ship was damaged or in difficulty.*

6 *They had lights on their helmets.*

7 *He thought they would soon have the ship working again.*

8 *Its eyes glowed like suns.*

9–10 *Suitable answers might mention the hideous sound it made, the way the ground trembled, the way it leapt at them, its jaws gaping open, the way the passengers needed to run for safety.*

11–13 Ben and his friend went to London last Thursday.

14–18 They went to London Zoo and Oxford Street.

19–23

	+er	+est
cold	colder	coldest
tall	taller	tallest
fast	faster	fastest

24 "Help, I'm stuck in the mud!" <u>screamed</u> Nasar.

25 "Where are you going?" Miss Thornton <u>asked</u>.

26 "Look at the clown!" <u>giggled</u> Caroline.

27 "I can't find my swimming costume," Joe <u>complained</u>.

28 *dash, sprint, jog*

29 *munch, scoff, nibble*

30 *yell, shriek*

Paper 6

1 moaning
2 say
3 cloudy
4 danced
5 *The gardener or Timothy*
6 *He was laughing*
7 *The sound of ducks quacking can sound like laughter*
8 *Any of: upset, silly, wet, foolish*
9–10 large   <u>small</u>   <u>little</u>
11–12 <u>quick</u>   slow   <u>fast</u>
13–14 <u>sea</u>   <u>ocean</u>   beach
15 bright
16 sharp
17 rainy
18 scary
19 rough
20–26 Mum said that she would take Paul to London to buy some roller skates. They set off from Walton at nine o'clock.
27 snowman
28 *seaweed/seagrass*
29 pineapple
30 football

Paper 7

1 sugar and butter and lemon juice
2–3 Don't make the pan too hot. Don't let the bananas get too mushy.
4 Remove the crusts and cut into chunks.
5 *Any sensible answer, e.g. otherwise you would not get the toffee mixture all the way through the pudding.*
6 6
7 You should put it in the fridge for a short while first.
8–11 *Four words ending with the **ly** suffix, e.g. calmly.*
12 "Where are you going?" called Mum.
13 "Here we are," Tom shouted.
14 "It is over there!" yelled Sarah.
15 "Shh, Tuhil is asleep," Dad whispered.
16 "Quick, it is catching us!" Gemma screamed.

17 gates
18 tracks
19 bridges
20 rabbits
21 tractors
22 farms
23–24 3, 7
25–26 1, 6
27–28 5, 8
29–30 2, 4

Paper 8

1 the Dormouse
2 three sisters
3 the March Hare and the Hatter
4–5 *Two of: They lived at the bottom of a well. They lived on treacle. It was a treacle-well.*
6 Polite
7 *Because she kept interrupting/didn't believe his story.*
8 Yes. *Because she wanted the story to go on/she enjoyed the fact that it was about eating and drinking.*
9 *went*
10 *took*
11 *planted/grew*
12 *Wash*
13 *saw/fed*
14 *drank*
15 5
16 3
17 1
18 6
19 2
20 4
21 helicopter
22 lorry
23 ship
24 train
25 **k**not
26 **w**rap
27 clim**b**
28 **w**riggly
29 com**b**
30 **k**nee

Paper 9

1 chips
2 frosty
3 a paper bag
4 *Vinegar and salt*
5 *To stop them burning his/her lips because the chips were hot*
6 *They were as 'slippery as a slide'*
7–9 three of: *raindrops, snowflakes, frosty, hot, warm*
10–14 France, Monday, Henry, India, Julia
15 out
16 cold
17 last
18 easy
19 *small/little*
20 don't
21 can't
22 we've
23 we're
24 it's
25 didn't
26 yellow
27 smelly
28–29 long, pretty
30 huge

Paper 10

1 in the barn
2 to stop it getting dusty
3 to go to college
4–6 Ploughing, tilling, mowing.
7 *Someone who is happy/used to living in a town and is not interested in the countryside.*
8 *He disliked the countryside. He only liked the town.*
9 flock
10 choir
11 herd
12 bunch

13–18

Expression of greeting	Expression of warning
Hello.	Watch out!
How are you?	Mind your head!
Good to see you.	Take care!

19 Be quiet!
20 What is your name?
21 Help!
22 Hurry up!
23 Do you want to watch a video?
24 Is it big?
25 uneven
26 disobey
27 disappear
28 untie
29 unhappy
30 disagree

Paper 11

1 Norway, Denmark
2 trading
3 north-west
4 when there were no sons
5 Silk, wine and jewellery.
6 *They were wealthy. They were badly defended.*
7 *The Vikings of Norway.*
8 *There was not much good farmland in their own countries.*
9–11 I'd like cheese, tomatoes, lettuce, pickle and ham on my sandwich.
12–13 Dad went shopping to buy a loaf of bread, some batteries, a bar of soap and a screwdriver.
14–15 At school we did maths, played football, painted a picture and read a book.
16 catch – caught
17 make – made
18 go – went
19 run – ran
20 drink – drank
21–26 other, wise, her, is, the, he

27 bus

28 lorry

29 coach

30 *vehicle*

Paper 12

1 slippers

2 what he bought the slippers for

3 no

4 *The dinosaur's paw was sore*

5 *roar*

6 *Answer stating what they think the dinosaur's teeth were for, e.g. I think the dinosaur's teeth were for eating children.*

7 *Answer stating what they would have done if they had met a dinosaur in a shoe-store, e.g. If I met a dinosaur in a shoe-store I would run away as fast as possible.*

8 apples

9 churches

10 boxes

11 pianos

12 cakes

13 ducklings

14 "Come here!" called David.

15 "What time is it?" asked Bethan.

16 "Let's take Snowy for a walk," Nasar suggested.

17 "Please can I have a cake?" asked Rupa.

18 "Where are you going?" called Mr Davenport.

19 "Look at the swans," called Jess excitedly.

20 "What a lovely morning!" exclaimed Frank.

21 saddle

22 scarf

23 shell

24 splash

25 storm

26 He

27 They

28–29 it, her

30 They

Paper 13

1 a film was about to start

2 eggs, bacon

3 because the shops were about to shut

4 *She was too young. She might be mugged or kidnapped.*

5 *She ran to fetch the shopping basket.*

6 *Answers that suggest that this is a remark about Lizzie's character and behaviour, e.g. she was very naughty, she would make the man turn grey with worry.*

7 *She was a receptionist in a local hotel. She addressed envelopes and delivered things.*

8 *Mrs Green did all the work/made the sandwiches while Mr Green did nothing.*

9 cutting

10 writing

11 running

12 riding

13 putting

14–19 HAIR – short, curly
SKIN – freckled, pale
EYES – bright, kind

20 *clean*

21 *out*

22 *rest/unemployment*

23 *bottom*

24 *difficult*

25 *young/new*

26 ?

27 ?

28 !

29 ?

30 !

Paper 14

1   a bow and two swords
2   its surroundings
3   we don't know
4   It was curiously carved.
5   *It was warm and sunny.*
6   *The snake burst/popped.*
7   *Because he did not run away when he saw the snake.*
8   *Because the dwarf admired his bravery.*
9   g**h**ost
10 s**w**ord
11 **k**nee
12 bom**b**
13 **k**night
14 s**c**issors
15 Although tired and hungry**,** Tuhil struggled on.
16 When you hear the bell**,** go outside.
17 Hot and panting**,** Hannah ran to catch the bus.
18 Monty sprinted down the valley**,** jumping the trickling stream.
19–22 salmon, spacecraft, deer, sheep
23 ladder – *equipment used for climbing things*
24 adult – *a grown-up person*
25 saddle – *a seat used on a horse or bike*
26 canoe – *a small light boat*
27 Fran**ce**
28 S**c**otland
29 **Ch**ina
30 Bra**z**il

Paper 15

1   two-thirds
2   five
3   giant squid, whales
4   the deep sea angler
5   During the day.
6   *It makes them almost invisible. They live in the dark zone.*
7   *Clever*
8   *So that it can swallow fish twice its size.*
9   *She shouted loudly.*

10 *He feels cold.*
11 *He talks all the time.*
12 *She is in a hurry.*
13 *She is hungry.*
14 *They will swim quickly.*
15 ours
16 mine
17 yours
18 hers
19–20 sleepier, sleepiest
21–22 funnier, funniest
23–24 smellier, smelliest
25–26 messier, messiest
27 *shouted*
28 *screamed*
29 *moaned*
30 *called*

Paper 16

1–4 Superbroom lets you do stunts in the air. It has two airbags. It is powered by batteries. There is a place for spell books.
5   *Two of: safety harness, disc brakes, windscreen wipers, dual airbags.*
6   At www.superbrooms.com.
7   Batteries
8   *The advice at the end tells you that you should always wear a helmet.*
9   afternoon
10 buttercup
11 armpit
12 toothache

Proper nouns	Common nouns	Collective nouns
Birmingham	spider	swarm
Wednesday	chair	team
Matthew	seaweed	herd

22–23 Farm Animals
24–26 Dexter the Mad Dog
27 *Goodbye.*
28 *Watch out!*
29 *Excuse me.*
30 *Thank you.*

Bond Assessment Papers: First papers in English

Paper 17

1 muddy
2 it travels quickly through air
3 he smacked his lips
4 leave some fish for him
5 *He did not say anything.*
6 *He did not want to abandon his fish.*
7 *Delicious/nice to eat.*
8 *Any sensible answer drawn from the story, e.g. that the lion was being unfair or a bully.*
9 lantern
10 lemonade
11 lifeboat
12 lollipop
13 luggage
14–22

male	female	plural
his	she	them
he	hers	ours
him	her	they

23 some, time, me, met, so
24 the, her, he, here
25 be, cause, us, use
26 with, in, it, thin, wit
27–30 The farmer stopped and looked at the goat in his garden, which was the fattest goat he'd ever seen. The goat had eaten the cabbages, carrots, runner beans, turnips and even the farmer's shirt off the washing line!

Paper 18

1 twenty thousand
2 go round the station
3 producer
4 *He had to text all six lucky numbers.*
5 *One and a half hours.*
6 Sunday
7 There is no phone number.
8 lovely
9 thankful
10 useful
11 honestly

12 careful
13 slowly
14–15 The men crossed the roads.
16–17 The children waited at the bus-stops.
18–19 The dogs sat under the trees.
20–21 The policemen ran to help the women.
22 First
23 *Then*
24 *Afterwards*
25 Finally
26 clean – dirty
27 correct – incorrect
28 honest – dishonest
29 there – here
30 difficult – easy

Paper 19

1 cold
2 labelled it
3 the smell of salt
4 it turned to mist
5 *Carefully, cautiously.*
6 *She thought he was far too secretive.*
7 *The cry of a sea bird.*
8 *It turned into a ship.*
9 *He felt fear or surprise.*
10–11 The (pretty) girl ran towards her friend.
12–13 Sid, the (miserable) lion, just growled.
14–15 David tiptoed down the (wooden) stairs.
16–17 The (old) man chuckled to himself.
18 remain
19 stretch
20 create
21 remove
22 are
23 am
24 is
25 am
26 I am
27 have not
28 was not
29 you have
30 would not

Bond Assessment Papers: First papers in English

1 gloves
2 in lines
3 about two minutes
4 *For wrapping Christmas and birthday presents.*
5 *It does not say.*
6 *They tell you that you must have an adult with you.*
7 Swirly patterns.
8 *Any sensible answer, e.g. give quantities of oil and white spirit to use.*
9–17 Judy wasn't scared about the wind rattling the windows. She snuggled up into her soft, warm, comfortable bed. "Are you all right?" she called out to her brother.

18 yours
19 I
20 They
21 she
22 smoke – clouds of gas and small bits of solid material
23 reptile – a cold-blooded animal
24 nostril – the two openings at the end of your nose
25 unclear
26 fairly
27 goodness
28 thoughtful
29 disappear
30 mistrust

The Vikings

The Vikings first came from Denmark, Norway and Sweden – the
lands we call Scandinavia. After the year 790, many Vikings left these
homelands and sailed east, west, south and north. Suddenly, it seemed
as if the Vikings were everywhere.   5

Traders, raiders, settlers, explorers

Vikings from different lands sailed for different reasons.
   Swedish Vikings were mainly interested in trade. They travelled east
and south across the rivers of Russia, taking walrus tusks, furs and slaves
down to the Black Sea. Here they traded them for silk, wine and jewellery.   10
   The Vikings of Denmark and Norway were traders too, but they found
it easier to get rich by raiding. They learned that lands to the west and
south were wealthy and badly defended. They attacked the coasts of
Europe, stealing treasure and capturing slaves. Later, they sailed back to
the British Isles and Northern France, to conquer land and to settle down.   15
   The Vikings of Norway were also explorers, looking for unknown lands.
They sailed north-west and found lands which they called Iceland and
Greenland. Norwegian Vikings then became the first Europeans to reach
North America.

Why did the Vikings appear?   20

People have suggested many reasons why the Vikings left home and
suddenly appeared off the coasts of Europe in the 790s.
   One important reason was that there was not much good farmland in
their own countries. When a Viking farmer died, his eldest son took over
the farm. Then the younger sons had to leave and look for somewhere   25
else to make a living. (Women only took over the farm if there were no sons.)

From *Vikings* by Peter Chrisp

Underline the right answers.

1 Which of these countries did Vikings come from?
(Finland, Norway, Ireland, Holland, Denmark)

2 Swedish Vikings were mainly interested in (raiding, exploring, trading, settling).

3 In which direction did the Norwegian Vikings explore?
(south-east, north-east, north-west, south-west)

4 When did Viking women take over farms?
(when the farmer died, when the younger son left, when the older son left, when there were no sons)

4

Answer these questions.

5 What things did Swedish Vikings bring back from the Black Sea?

_____

6 Give two reasons why Vikings wanted to raid the lands to the west and south.

(1) _____

(2) _____

7 Who discovered Iceland and Greenland?

_____

8 Give one reason why the Vikings suddenly appeared off the coasts of Europe in the 790s.

_____

4

Add the missing commas (,).

9–11 I'd like cheese tomatoes lettuce pickle and ham on my sandwich.

12–13 Dad went shopping to buy a loaf of bread some batteries a bar of soap and a screwdriver.

14–15 At school we did maths played football painted a picture and read a book.

7

With a line match the **present** and **past tenses** of these **verbs**.

16 catch   made

17 make   drank

18 go   caught

19 run   went

20 drink   ran

( ) 5

Write all the small words you can find in the word *otherwise*.

21–26 _____   _____   _____

_____   _____   _____

( ) 6

Find the hidden words in questions 27–29 and then complete question 30.

27 chbusdf   _____

28 hlorrybnds   _____

29 nkgdjcoacht   _____

30 All the hidden words are types of _____.

( ) 4

Now go to the Progress Chart to record your score!   Total ( ) 30

Paper 12

Dinosaur Stomp

I thought I saw
a dinosaur
buy a pair of slippers
in a big shoe-store
I asked him what   5
he bought them for
and he told me
his paw was sore
and what's more
began to roar   10
and showed me what
his teeth were for.

I ran like mad
across the floor
and bolted through   15
the shoe-store door
and nevermore
no nevermore
laughed out loud
at a dinosaur.   20

by David Harmer

Underline the right answers.

1 What was the dinosaur buying in the big shoe-store?
   (slippers, shoes, boots)

2 What did the child ask the dinosaur?
   (if he felt all right, what he bought the slippers for, what his teeth were
   for)

3 After leaving the shop did the child ever laugh at a dinosaur again?
   (yes, no, don't know)

Answer these questions.

4 Why did the dinosaur need a pair of slippers?

_____

5 Which word describes the sound the dinosaur made?

_____

6 The dinosaur showed the child 'what his teeth were for'. What do you
   think his teeth were for?

_____

7 What would you have done if you had met a dinosaur in a shoe-store?

_____ ◯ 4

Write the **plural** of each of these **nouns**.

8 apple _____   **9** church _____

10 box _____   **11** piano _____

12 cake _____   **13** duckling _____ ◯ 6

Add the missing speech marks (" ") before and after what has actually been said.

14 Come here! called David.

15 What time is it? asked Bethan.

16 Let's take Snowy for a walk, Nasar suggested.

17 Please can I have a cake? asked Rupa.

18 Where are you going? called Mr Davenport.

19 Look at the swans, called Jess excitedly.

20 What a lovely morning! exclaimed Frank. ◯ 7

Write these words in **alphabetical order**.

shell   scarf   storm   splash   saddle

21 (1) _____   **22** (2) _____

23 (3) _____   **24** (4) _____

25 (5) _____ ◯ 5

Cross out the words in bold and write the correct **pronoun** for each question.

26 **James** was painting a picture. _____

27 **Annie and Tim** were playing in a puddle. _____

28–29 Watch out, **the stone** might hit **Jenny** on the head. _____

30 **The chickens** lay lots of eggs. _____ ◯ 5

Paper 13

'Go and do some shopping for me, please, you two!' said Lizzie's mum. Lizzie's brother Tom groaned. He was very busy lying on the sofa and drinking a can of coke.

'Oh, Mum!' he said. 'That Buster Keaton film is on in a minute! Why can't she go on her own?'   5

'I'm too young,' said Lizzie, bouncing off the armchair and running for the shopping basket. 'I might get mugged or kidnapped by a desperate man with a black beard.'

'Ten minutes with you and his beard would turn grey,' said Tom, moving one leg idly off the sofa.   10

'Oh, come on, Tom,' said Mrs Green. 'If you want any breakfast tomorrow you'll have to go and get it. Here's the list: bacon, eggs, butter and coffee. I haven't got time to go myself: I've got all these envelopes to address. Get a move on! The shops'll be shut in ten minutes.'

Tom and Lizzie's mother worked very hard. In the daytime she was a   15
receptionist at the local hotel; in the evening, sometimes, she addressed envelopes and delivered things. She ran everywhere, she was always tired, and she never had enough time. She even made sandwiches for Dad, whilst he sat and stared out of the window. Lizzie did not think this was quite fair.   20

She loved her dad very much, though Mr Green worked in a garage. He always came home covered in oil.

From *Chicken Mission* by Sue Limb

34

Underline the correct answers.

1 Why did Tom say he didn't want to go to the shops?
   (he was lying on the sofa, a film was about to start, he was drinking a coke)

2 Which of these things were on the shopping list?
   (coke, bread, eggs, tea, bacon)

3 Why was it important for the children to go straight away?
   (to stop them being so lazy, because there was nothing for supper, because the shops were about to shut)

3

Answer these questions.

4 What two reasons did Lizzie give for not wanting to go to the shops alone?

   (1) _____

   (2) _____

5 How can you tell Lizzie would quite like to go to the shops?

   _____

6 In line 9, Tom says, 'Ten minutes with you and his beard would turn grey.' What is he really saying about Lizzie?

   _____

7 What two jobs did Mrs Green do?

   (1) _____

   (2) _____

8 Why was it not fair that Mr Green just sat and stared out of the window?

   _____

   _____

   _____

5

Add *ing* to the **verb** at the beginning of each line to finish the sentence. Don't forget any spelling changes.

9 cut   Michael is _____ his birthday cake.

10 write David is _____ a letter to his friend.

11 run   Caroline is _____ up the garden path.

12 ride   Susan is _____ a donkey on the beach.

13 put   Tony is _____ on his swimming trunks.

◯ 5

Put the **adjectives** in the correct columns.

       bright   freckled   short   kind   pale   curly

14–19 HAIR   SKIN   EYES

_____   _____   _____

_____   _____   _____

◯ 6

Write the **antonym** of each word.

20 dirty   _____   **21** in   _____

22 work   _____   **23** top   _____

24 easy   _____   **25** old   _____

◯ 6

Add a question mark (?) or exclamation mark (!).

26 Where can I buy an ice-cream_____

27 Is it time yet_____

28 Hurry up or we will be late_____

29 Why do I have to wear this hat_____

30 Run_____

◯ 5

This story is set in Japan. It is about a warrior called Fujiwara-san.

One day, when he was travelling alone in the mountains with his bow on
his back and his two sharp swords in his belt, he came to the curiously
carved bridge of Karashi which spanned one end of the beautiful lake
Biwa. It was a lake famous for the flowering trees which lined its banks   5
and for the snow-capped mountains reflected in its surface.

    Fujiwara-san was about to cross the bridge when he noticed that a
large serpent was coiled in the middle of the centre arch basking in the
warm sunshine. It was the biggest snake he had ever seen, seven or
eight metres long at least, and at the young warrior's approach it instantly   10
reared its head. It kept still for a minute then, as Fujiwara-san advanced
towards it, it suddenly uncoiled and stretched its length across the bridge
in such a way that no one could cross without treading on its scaly body.

    Ordinary men would have taken to their heels at so frightening a sight,
but Fujiwara-san was no ordinary man. Buckling his sword belt on tighter   15
he strode straight ahead, not pausing for so much as a second as he
reached the ugly creature, walking across it with a *crunch! squash!
crunch! squash!* before turning and giving it a kick. As he did so it blurted
a gush of hot air like a slashed balloon, rapidly becoming smaller and
smaller and then disappeared. Where the serpent had been there now   20
crouched a tiny dwarf, a little man of uncertain age who was so intent on
bowing so low to the young warrior that his head touched the planks of
the bridge, not once but three times.

From *The Shining Princess* by Eric Quayle and Michael Foreman

Underline the right answers.

1 Fujiwara-san carried (a sword and an axe, a bow and a spear, a bow and two swords).

2 What was the lake famous for?
(its colour, its fish, its surroundings)

3 How old was the dwarf?
(old, young, we don't know)

3

Answer these questions.

4 What was special about the bridge over the lake?

_____

5 What was the weather like?

_____

6 Say, in your own words, what happened to the snake as Fujiwara-san walked over it.

_____

7 Why was Fujiwara-san not an ordinary man?

_____

8 Why do you think the dwarf bowed to Fujiwara-san ?

_____

5

Add the missing silent letters.

9 g__ost

10 s__ord

11 __nee

12 bom__

13 __night

14 s__issors

6

Add a comma (,) to each sentence to show where a short pause is needed.

15 Although tired and hungry Tuhil struggled on.

16 When you hear the bell go outside.

17 Hot and panting Hannah ran to catch the bus.

18 Monty sprinted down the valley jumping the trickling stream.

4

Circle the **nouns** whose **singular** and **plural** forms are the same.

19–22 horse   salmon   spacecraft

deer   knife   sheep

4

Write a short **definition** for each word.

23 ladder   _____

24 adult   _____

25 saddle   _____

26 canoe   _____

4

Add the missing **vowel letters** to each word to make a country.

27 Fr__nc__   **28** Sc__tl__nd

29 Ch__n__   **30** Br__z__l

4

Now go to the Progress Chart to record your score!   Total   30

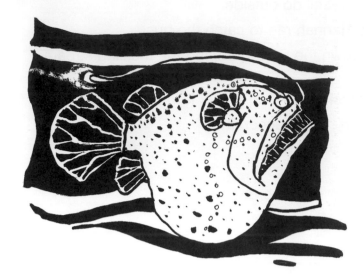

The deep sea

We live surrounded by water. Two-thirds of the Earth's surface is covered
by sea water. Ninety-seven per cent of all water on the planet is salty.

The Earth's five oceans are home to a huge variety of plants and
animals, living at many different depths. The top 200 metres of the sea   5
receive light from the Sun that allows plants to grow. All the fish that we
eat live at this depth, as well as turtles and jellyfish.

Below this lies the twilight zone, where giant squid and some whales
lurk. Many of the fish at this level come up to the surface at night to feed.
In this way they can avoid being attacked by daytime hunters such as   10
sea birds.

At 3300 metres the dark zone starts. There is no light here at all, and
the water is extremely cold, about 1–2° centigrade. Many of the fish
at this level are also black, making them almost invisible. They have
ingenious ways of catching prey. The anglerfish has a light on its nose   15
to attract other fish to it. The umbrella mouth gulper swims along with its
large mouth open wide like a fishing net, hoping to scoop up passing
creatures. The deep sea angler has razor sharp teeth and a stretchy
stomach that allows it to swell up like an enormous ball. It can expand to
eat a fish twice its size, which it swallows whole without chewing.   20

The bottom of the sea is very varied. There are mountains, plains and
valleys, and trenches that are deeper than the height of Mount Everest.
Because it is impossible for humans to reach these depths by submarine,
they are very difficult to explore. It is certain that they contain many life
forms still waiting to be discovered.   25

Underline the right answers.

1 How much of the Earth's surface is sea?
(a third, a half, a quarter, two-thirds, a fifth)

2 How many oceans are there?
(one, two, three, four, five)

3 Which of these creatures live in the twilight zone?
(giant squid, sharks, turtles, whales, jellyfish)

4 Which fish has sharp teeth?
(the giant squid, the umbrella mouth gulper, the deep sea angler, the anglerfish)

4

Answer these questions.

5 When do sea birds look for food?

_____

6 Why do you think so many fish below 3300 metres are black?

_____

7 What does 'ingenious' in line 15 mean?

_____

8 Explain in your own words why the deep sea angler has a stretchy stomach.

_____

4

Rewrite each sentence as if you are writing about someone else.

e.g.   I enjoy painting.   She enjoys painting.

9 I shouted loudly.   _____

10 I feel cold.   _____

11 I talk all the time.   _____

12 I am in a hurry.   _____

13 I am hungry.   _____

14 I will swim quickly.   _____

6

Underline the **possessive pronoun** in each sentence.

15 "That car isn't as good as ours."

16 "Sam's hair isn't as long as mine."

17 "Jack's bike goes faster than yours."

18 "That T-shirt is nicer than hers."

4

Add *er* and *est* to the words in bold. Remember a letter needs to change each time!

19–20 **sleepy** _____   _____

21–22 **funny** _____   _____

23–24 **smelly** _____   _____

25–26 **messy** _____   _____

8

Fill in the gaps with four different **dialogue words**.

27 "I promise I will be quick," Ahmed _____.

28 "Run! David is catching you," _____ Clare.

29 Ben _____, "I hate mashed potato."

30 "Please go and play for a minute," _____ Mum.

4

Now go to the Progress Chart to record your score!   Total   30

New! Superbroom!

Superbroom is the new must-have gadget – a high-performance electronic broom that leaves all the others standing.

With Superbroom you can do all the top stunts it takes years to learn at wizard school:

- loop the loops
- vertical take-offs
- figure-of-eights
- hovering and gliding.

Superbroom has the following features for maximum performance:

- 2 wolfpower engines
- safety harness
- disc brakes
- cat basket
- 4 speed windscreen wipers
- glove compartment for spell books
- dual airbags
- runs off rechargeable batteries.*

Superbroom ... it's just magic!

£199.99

www.superbrooms.com

*batteries not included

It is always best to wear a helmet when riding Superbroom.

5

10

15

20

1–4 Look at these sentences below about the advertisement.
Four are true, the others are not. Underline the true sentences.

Superbroom lets you do stunts in the air.

It costs more than two hundred pounds.

It has two airbags.

It has a double exhaust pipe.

It is powered by batteries.

It allows you to go to wizard school.

You can't see in the rain.

There is a place for spell books.

4

Answer these questions.

5 List two safety features of the Superbroom.

(1) _____ (2) _____

6 Where can you find out more about Superbroom?

_____

7 What is not included with Superbroom?

_____

8 Which piece of information might make you think that Superbroom is quite dangerous?

_____

4

Use a word from the box to finish each **compound word**.

ache	cup	noon	pit

9 after_____ **10** butter_____

11 arm_____ **12** tooth_____

4

Sort the **nouns** into the correct columns in the table below.

13–21 Birmingham   spider   chair   Wednesday

swarm   Matthew   team

herd   seaweed

Proper nouns	Common nouns	Collective nouns

9

Capital letters are used for all the important words in book titles.
Copy these book titles, adding the missing capital letters.

22–23 farm animals   _____

24–26 dexter the mad dog   _____

5

Write another way of saying . . .

27 See you soon.   _____

28 Beware!   _____

29 Pardon me.   _____

30 That is very kind of you.   _____

4

Now go to the Progress Chart to record your score!   Total   30

Paper 17

One day Spider went to the river to fish. It must have been Spider's lucky day, for the fish swarmed around him until at last he had a large pile lying on the muddy river bank beside him.

'Now for a fire to cook my supper,' exclaimed Spider in delight, and quickly collecting a few sticks, he made a fire and began roasting his fish. 5

As everybody knows, the smell of roasting fish is not only delicious but it travels quickly through the air, and so it happened that a passing lion stopped in his tracks, sniffed appreciatively once or twice and followed his nose.

He found Spider just about to eat the first of the fish he had cooked, 10 and roared, 'give that to me,' so fiercely, that Spider handed it over without a word.

'Delicious!' exclaimed the lion, smacking his lips and half-closing his eyes, while he sat down by the fire and said, 'Now cook me some more!'

Spider was too frightened of the large, fierce lion even to think of 15 disobeying him and he certainly could not run away without abandoning all his fish. So he set to work to cook some more, hoping that the lion would soon have had enough and that there would be a few left for him. After all, he had done all the hard work and was aching with hunger.

One by one the savoury, sweet-smelling fish disappeared down the 20 lion's throat while poor Spider was run off his feet collecting firewood.

From *African Myths and Legends* by Kathleen Arnott

Underline the right answers.

1 What was the river bank like?
   (hot, wet, muddy)

2 What is special about the smell of roasting fish?
(it travels quickly through air, it is unpleasant, it lasts a long time)

3 How did the lion show his enjoyment of the fish?
(he sat down by the fire, he smacked his lips, he roared at Spider)

4 What did Spider hope that the lion would do?
(give him some fish back, leave some fish for him, go to sleep)

4

Answer these questions.

5 What did Spider say when the lion demanded his fish?

_____

6 Why did Spider not run away from the lion?

_____

7 What does 'savoury' mean in line 20?

_____

8 What do you think Spider felt about the lion's behaviour?

_____

_____

4

Write these words in **alphabetical order**.

lifeboat   lemonade   lantern   luggage   lollipop

9 (1) _____   **10** (2) _____

11 (3) _____   **12** (4) _____

13 (5) _____

5

Complete the table of **pronouns**.

his   she   hers   them   he   him   ours   they   her

14–22

male	female	plural

9

(47)

What hidden words can be found in these words?

23 sometime _____ _____ _____ _____ _____

24 there _____ _____ _____ _____

25 because _____ _____ _____ _____

26 within _____ _____ _____ _____ _____

4

Add the missing commas.

27–30 The farmer stopped and looked at the goat in his garden which was the fattest goat he'd ever seen. The goat had eaten the cabbages carrots runner beans turnips and even the farmer's shirt off the washing line!

4

Now go to the Progress Chart to record your score!   Total

30

LiveTV
Vision House
Belleway
London
EC7 8ZU

5

18 October 2007

Dear Jack Taylor

Lucky winner!

I am writing to you from LiveTV. I am delighted to let you know that you have won the golden ticket prize in our 'Meet the Stars' Competition.

10

I can't tell you how excited we are by this event. You were the only entrant to text all the six lucky numbers – and we had 20,000 replies.

So on Saturday 21 November you will be the guest at our show. You will get the chance to meet the Number 1 hit band, the Snowstorms and to appear on stage with them. We will send a taxi to pick you and your parents up at 2pm and get you to the studio at 3.30pm. Before the show we will take you round the TV station. The show is being recorded at 5pm and takes an hour. It will be shown at 9pm the following night.

15

20

After the recording we will take you out to dinner at the Glitz hotel. We will put you and your parents up for the night in the hotel. A taxi will take you all home the next morning.

25

Just phone my assistant Tricia and she will explain all the details. Looking forward to seeing you there!

Best wishes

Jane Thompson
'Meet the Stars' Producer

30

Underline the right answers.

1 How many people entered the competition?
(one thousand, twenty thousand, five hundred)

2 What will Jack do when he first gets to LiveTV?
(meet the Snowstorms, go round the station, go on stage)

3 What is Jane Thompson's job?
(producer, director, actor)

3

Answer these questions.

4 What did Jack have to do to win the competition?

_____

5 How long does it take from Jack's house to LiveTV?

_____

6 Which day of the week will 'Meet the Stars' be shown on?

_____

7 Why does the letter make it hard for Jack to phone Tricia?

_____

4

Add the **suffix** *ful* or *ly* to each word.

8 love_____   9 thank_____   10 use_____

11 honest_____   12 care_____   13 slow_____

6

Rewrite these sentences, changing them from **singular** to **plural**.

14–15 The man crossed the road.

_____

16–17 The child waited at the bus-stop.

_____

18–19 The dog sat under the tree.

_____

20–21 The policeman ran to help the woman.

_____ **8**

Fill each gap with a word that shows the sequence of events.

Then   Finally   First   Afterwards

22 _____ put toothpaste on your toothbrush.

23 _____ brush your teeth.

24 _____ you can rinse your mouth with water.

25 _____ get into bed. **4**

Draw a line to match the **antonyms**.

26 clean   dishonest

27 correct   easy

28 honest   dirty

29 there   incorrect

30 difficult   here **5**

Paper 19

William finds his grandfather's old trunk and opens it.

And there, inside the trunk, lying on rotting sacks, was an old bottle. An old green bottle. Made of glass, but of a glass so ancient and dark and pitted that William could not begin to guess what might be hidden inside it.

Gingerly he rolled it over on the sacking. It felt chill to the touch. What was inside? As Granny said, his grandfather was far too secretive. He should have labelled it. Then William would not have had to lift it out – oh, so carefully – and hold it, colder than a stone in his hand, while he twisted at the encrusted glass stopper. What was it Grandfather always said when he chose to keep a secret?

'That's between me and Mustapha.'

Such a curious thing to say. So foreign and exotic. And suddenly William found himself softly saying the word aloud, testing the strangeness out on his own tongue.

'Mustapha.'

Then, just a little louder.

'Mustapha.'

Then, louder still:

'Mustapha. Mustapha. *Mustapha!*'

There was another swirl of icy wind. The smell of salt grew stronger, and William could have sworn he heard the lonely cry of a sea bird. The room started to heave, as if the floorboards had become a ship's deck, and the storeroom itself was suddenly afloat on the high seas.

Then, with a crack, the stopper of the bottle split in two. Each half of shattered glass began to melt into a mist, green as the bottle itself. And from the bottle poured more mist, and more and more, until it was as thick as fog, and a green pillar of it coiled and rose, up and up, higher and higher, until it was as high as the ceiling.

From *A Sudden Swirl of Icy Wind* by Anne Fine

1 The bottle felt (warm, cold, wet).

2 What should Grandfather have done with the bottle?
(labelled it, sold it, opened it)

3 What smell entered the room?
(the smell of dust, the smell of salt, the smell of fish)

4 What happened to the stopper of the bottle?
(it bounced on the floor, it rolled away, it turned to mist)

4

Answer these questions.

5 What does 'gingerly' in line 5 mean?

_____

6 What did Granny think was wrong with William's grandfather?

_____

7 What did William hear after he called Mustapha's name?

_____

8 What did the room seem to turn into?

_____

9 How do you think William felt when the green mist came out?

_____

5

Underline the **verbs** and circle the **adjectives** in each sentence.

10–11 The pretty girl ran towards her friend.

12–13 Sid, the miserable lion, just growled.

14–15 David tiptoed down the wooden stairs.

16–17 The old man chuckled to himself.

8

Match the **synonyms**.

stretch   remain   create   remove

18 _____ = stay   19 _____ = lengthen

20 _____ = make   21 _____ = take away

4

53

Add the missing word to make the sentence make sense and put in the **present tense**.

22 "We _____ waiting!" called the children.

23 "I _____ ready," replied Mum.

24 "Where _____ Billy?" she asked.

25 "I _____ coming!" he shouted.

Write the two words each word is made from.

26 I'm = _____ _____   27 haven't = _____ _____

28 wasn't = _____ _____   29 you've = _____ _____

30 wouldn't = _____ _____

Now go to the Progress Chart to record your score!   Total   30

How to make marbled wrapping paper

Marbled paper makes a lovely wrapping for
Christmas and birthday presents.

You need

* A plastic tray filled with water

* Oil paints mixed with white spirit

* A straw

* White paper

 You must do this with an adult

1 Take the tray filled with water. Pour on the oil
  and water mixture in lines.
2 Draw the straw across the surface of the
  mixture in opposite directions to make swirly
  patterns.
3 Carefully lay a piece of paper on the surface.
  Leave it for a couple of minutes.
4 Peel it off and leave it to dry. You have a sheet
  of marbled patterned paper.

Underline the right answers.

1 Which of these things do you not need for paper marbling?
(paper, white spirit, water, gloves, a straw)

2 How should you pour in the oil and water mixture?
(in swirls, in lines, in zigzags)

3 How long do you need to leave the paper in the tray?
(about one minute, about ten minutes, about two minutes)

3

Answer these questions.

4 What can you use marbled paper for?

_____

5 How much paint and white spirit do you need to use?

_____

6 What safety advice do the instructions give you?

_____

7 What kind of patterns can you get on the paper?

_____

8 How do you think these instructions could be improved?

_____

5

Copy the passage and add the missing punctuation.

9-17 Judy wasnt scared about the wind rattling the windows She snuggled
up into her soft warm comfortable bed Are you all right she called out
to her brother

_____

_____

_____

_____

_____

9

Circle the **pronouns** in each sentence.

18 Is this cat yours?

19 I love cheese on toast.

20 They are always late.

21 Where has she gone?

With a line match each word with its **definition**.

22 smoke   a cold-blooded animal

23 reptile   clouds of gas and small bits of solid material

24 nostril   the two openings at the end of your nose   **3**

Underline the **prefix** or **suffix** in each word.

25 unclear   **26** fairly   **27** goodness

28 thoughtful   **29** disappear   **30** mistrust   **6**

Now go to the Progress Chart to record your score!   **Total**   **30**

Progress Chart   First papers in English

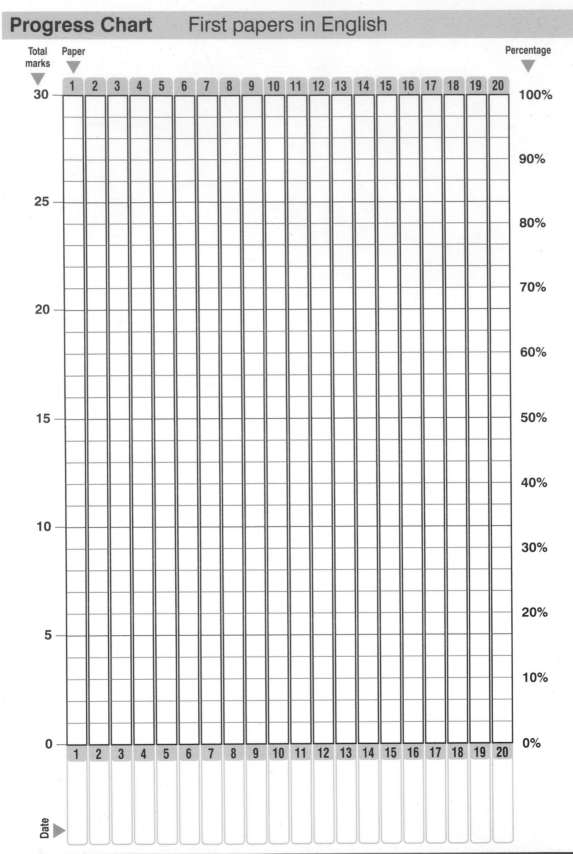

Total marks ▼

Paper ▼

Percentage ▼

When you've finished the book read the Next Steps ➤